Forgive and Build Bridges

JOHN BEVERE

Books about Spirit-Led Living

The Inner Strength Series
LIVING WITH STRENGTH IN TODAY'S WORLD

FORGIVE AND BUILD BRIDGES by John Bevere
Published by Charisma House
A part of Strang Communications Company
600 Rinehart Road
Lake Mary, Florida 32746
www.charismahouse.com

Unless otherwise noted, all Scripture quotations are from the New King James Version of the Bible. Copyright © 1979, 1980, 1982 by Thomas Nelson, Inc., publishers. Used by permission.

Cover design by Rachel Campbell

Library of Congress Catalog Card Number: 2001098129
International Standard Book Number: 0-88419-836-7

02 03 04 05   87654321
Printed in the United States of America

Contents

Introduction

The greatest gift any person can receive from God is the gift of His forgiveness from sin. Without forgiveness—available to everyone through God's gift of salvation in Christ Jesus—no one could escape the reality of hell because of sin.

In Titus 2:14 we are told that Jesus "gave Himself for us, that He might redeem us from every lawless deed and purify for Himself His own special people, zealous for good works." God's answer for our sin is salvation through His gift of grace. God's forgiveness for your sins—and mine—wiped the slate clean. With it, we stand purified and forgiven before Him as "His own special people."

But accepting God's forgiveness for our sins is not the whole picture. We must learn to forgive others just as Christ has forgiven us. A person who cannot forgive has forgotten how great a debt God has forgiven them.

Therefore I say to you, whatever things you ask when you pray, believe that you receive them, and you will have them. And whenever you stand praying, if you have anything against anyone, forgive him, that your Father in heaven may also forgive you your trespasses. But if you do not forgive, neither will your Father in heaven forgive your trespasses."

—Mark 11:24-26

Unless we can learn to let go of the offenses others have caused in our lives, freely and wholly forgiving them just as Christ has forgiven us, the Bible tells us that "neither will your Father in heaven forgive your trespasses."

We must learn to forgive others just as Christ has forgiven us.

In this book we will take a closer look at learning to forgive others so we can build a bridge to span the deep, dark chasm of offense. In some cases, those we forgive will be able to walk across this bridge to receive the gift of God's salvation for the first time. In other cases, we will discover that we can use that bridge ourselves to restore a broken relationship and live in the joy and peace of a reconciled relationship.

As you begin reading, ask the Holy Spirit to walk with you through your past, bringing before you any people against whom you have held something. Ask Him to enable you to forgive those offenses. Then read this book proactively—determining in advance that you will use the tools you find in it to build a bridge of reconciliation. Remember the words of Christ: "Forgive, and you will be forgiven" (Luke 6:37).

Now, read on and become a bridge builder!

ONE

Learning
to Forgive

DEVELOPING
Inner Strength

I heard an unusual testimony about a minister in the Philippines. Friends of mine who had known him from a previous ministry showed me an article telling about his experiences.

The man had resisted the call of God on his life for several years because of his business success. He was making a large amount of money. His disobedience eventually caught up with him, and he was rushed to the hospital because of heart failure.

He died on the operating table and found himself outside the gates of heaven. Jesus was standing there and dealt with him about his disobedience. The man pleaded with the Lord to extend his life. If the Lord would do so, the man promised he would serve Him. The Lord consented.

Before sending him back to his body, the Lord showed him a vision of hell. He saw his wife's mother burning in the flames of hell.

He was amazed. She had said the "sinner's prayer," confessed to being a Christian and had attended church. "Why is she in hell?" he asked the Lord.

The Lord told him that she had refused to forgive a relative and therefore could not be forgiven.

When Jesus said, "But if you do not forgive, neither will your Father in heaven forgive your trespasses," He meant what He said (Mark 11:26). We live in a culture where we don't always mean what we say. Consequently we do not believe others mean what they say to us. A person's word is not taken seriously.

It begins in childhood. A parent tells a child, "If you do that again, you'll get a spanking." The child not only does it again, but several times more after that. Following each episode the child receives the same warning from his parent. Usually no corrective action is taken. If correction does take place, it is either lighter than what was promised or more severe because the parent is frustrated.

Both responses send a message to the child that parents don't mean what they say or that what parents say isn't always true. The child learns to think that not everything authority figures say is true, so he becomes confused about when and if he should take authority figures seriously. This attitude is projected onto other areas of his life. He views his teachers, friends, leaders and bosses through this same frame of reference. By the time he becomes an adult he has accepted this as normal. His conversations now consist of promises and statements in which he says things he doesn't mean.

Let me give you a hypothetical example of a typical conversation. Jim sees Tom, whom he knows but hasn't talked to in a while. He is in a hurry and thinks, *Oh, no. I can't believe I am running into Tom. I don't have time to talk.*

The two men look at each other.

Jim says, "Praise the Lord, brother. It is good to see you."

They talk a short while. Since Jim is in a hurry, he finishes by saying, "We need to get together sometime for lunch."

In that short encounter, Jim did not say what he meant at least three times. First, although Jim was not excited about seeing Tom because he was in a hurry, he said to Tom, "Good to see you." Second, he was not really thinking about the Lord when he greeted Tom with, "Praise the Lord." Third, he had no intention of following up on that lunch invitation. It was just a means of getting away quicker and easing his conscience in the process. So Jim really meant nothing he said in that conversation.

Real situations like this occur every day. Today most people do not mean much of what they say. Is it any wonder we have a difficult time knowing when to take a person at his or her word?

But when Jesus speaks, He wants us to take Him seriously. We cannot view what He says the way we view the other authorities or relationships in our lives. When He says something, He means it. He is faithful even when we are faithless. He walks at a level of truth and integrity that transcends our culture or society. When Jesus said, "But if you do not forgive, neither will your Father in heaven forgive your trespasses," He meant it.

To take this one step further, He does not say this just once in the Gospels but many times. He was emphasizing the importance of this warning. Let's look at a few of these statements He made on different occasions.

> For if you forgive men their trespasses, your heavenly Father will also forgive you. But if you do not forgive men their trespasses, neither will your Father forgive your trespasses.
>
> —MATTHEW 6:14–15

And again:

> Forgive, and you will be forgiven.
>
> —Luke 6:37

Again in the Lord's Prayer we read:

> And forgive us our debts, *as we forgive* our debtors.
>
> —Matthew 6:12, emphasis added

I wonder how many Christians would want God to forgive them in the same way they have forgiven those who have offended them. Yet this is exactly the way in which they will be forgiven. Because unforgiveness is so rampant in our churches, we do not want to take these words of Jesus so seriously. Rampant or not, truth does not change. The way we forgive, release and restore another person is the way we will be forgiven.

Forgiveness and Spiritual Growth

We have seen many examples of unforgiveness in our own ministry. When I was ministering for the first time in Indonesia, I stayed in the home of a wealthy businessman. Even though he and his family attended the church where I was ministering, they were not saved.

During the week I was there, his wife was saved. He was next, and all three children followed. There was deliverance, and the entire atmosphere in the house was changed. Great joy filled their home.

When they learned I would be returning to Indonesia with my wife, they invited us to stay with them, offering to pay for the airline tickets of my children and a babysitter.

> When Jesus said,
> "But if you do not forgive,
> neither will your Father
> in heaven forgive your
> trespasses," He meant it.

We arrived and ministered ten times in their church. I preached on repentance and the presence of God. We sensed His presence in the services, with tears flowing and cries of deliverance throughout.

The entire family was again ministered to. The husband's mother, who lived in the same city, attended every service. She had also contributed a large amount of money to my children's airline tickets.

Near the end of the week, this man's mother looked me straight in the eye and asked, "John, why have I never felt the presence of God?"

We had just finished breakfast, and everyone else had already left the table.

"I have been to every service," she continued, "and have listened closely to everything you've said. I have come to the front repenting, yet I have not felt the presence of God once. Not only that, but I have never felt the presence of God at any other time, either."

I talked with her for a while and then said, "Let's pray for you to be filled with God's Spirit." I laid my hands upon her and prayed for her to receive the Holy Spirit, but there was no sense of God's presence at all.

Then God spoke to my spirit. "She is holding unforgiveness against her husband. Tell her to forgive him."

I took my hands off her. I knew her husband was dead, but I looked at her and said, "The Lord shows me you are holding unforgiveness against your husband."

"Yes, I am," she agreed. "But I have done my best to forgive him."

Then she told me about the horrible things he had done to her. I could see why she wrestled with forgiving him. But I said to her, "For you to receive from God you must forgive," and explained what Jesus taught about forgiveness.

The way we forgive, release and restore another person is the way we will be forgiven.

"You cannot forgive him in your own strength. You must take this before God and first ask God to forgive you. Then you can forgive your husband. Are you willing to release your husband?" I asked.

"Yes," she answered.

I led her in a simple prayer: "Father in heaven, in Jesus' name I ask Your forgiveness for holding unforgiveness against my husband. Lord, I know I cannot forgive him in my own strength. I have already failed, but before You now I release my husband from my heart. I forgive him."

No sooner had she said those words than tears began to flow down her cheeks. "Lift up your hands and speak in tongues," I urged her.

For the first time she prayed in a beautiful heavenly language. We had such a strong sense of the presence of the Lord at the breakfast table that we were overwhelmed and awed by it. She wept for about five minutes. We talked a little while, then I encouraged her to enjoy the presence of the Lord. She continued to worship Him, and I left her alone.

When news reached her son and daughter-in-law, they were shocked. The son said he had never seen his mother cry. She herself did not remember the last time she had cried. "Even when my husband died I did not cry," she said.

In the service that night she was baptized in water. For the next three days a glow and a sweet smile radiated from her face. I did not remember seeing her smile before that. Because she had been unwilling to forgive, she had been imprisoned by unforgiveness. But once she released her husband and forgave him, she received the power of the Lord in her life and became aware of His presence.

Adapted from John Bevere, *The Bait of Satan* (Lake Mary, FL: Charisma House, 1994, 1997), 129–134.

TWO

Lessons From an Unforgiving Servant

DEVELOPING
Inner Strength

In Matthew 18, Jesus sheds light on the bondage of unforgiveness and offense. Peter asked Him, "Lord, how often shall my brother sin against me, and I forgive him? Up to seven times?" (Matt. 18:21).

Peter liked to take things to the extreme. He was the one who had said, "Let us make three tabernacles: one for You, one for Moses, and one for Elijah" on the mountain of transfiguration (Matt. 17:4). Now he thought he was being magnanimous. "I'll impress the Master with my willingness to forgive seven times."

But he received a shocking reply. Jesus blew away what Peter considered generous:

> *I do not say to you, up to seven times, but*
> *up to seventy times seven.*
> —MATTHEW 18:22

In other words, forgive as God does, without limits.

When Jesus spoke to Peter about the importance of forgiving without limits, He wanted Peter to understand that important principle. In order to emphasize His words, Jesus told a parable to illustrate His point.

> Therefore the kingdom of heaven is like a certain king who wanted to settle accounts with his servants. And when he had begun to settle accounts, one was brought to him who owed him ten thousand talents.
> —MATTHEW 18:23–24

To understand the enormity of what Jesus was saying, we must know what a talent was. A *talent* was a unit of measure used to measure gold, silver and other metals and commodities. (See 2 Samuel 12:30; 1 Kings 20:39.) In this parable Jesus told, a talent represents a debt, so we can safely assume He was referring to a unit of exchange such as gold or silver. Let's say gold.

The common talent was equivalent to approximately seventy-five pounds. It was the full weight that a man could carry. (See 2 Kings 5:23.) Ten thousand talents would be approximately 750,000 pounds or 375 tons. So this servant owed the king 375 tons of gold.

At the present time, the price of gold is roughly $265 an ounce. In today's market a talent of gold would be worth $318,000. Therefore, ten thousand talents of gold are worth 3.2 billion dollars. This servant owed his king 3.2 billion dollars!

Jesus was emphasizing here that this servant owed a debt he could never pay. We read:

> But as he was not able to pay, his master commanded that he be sold, with his wife and children and all that he had, and that payment be made. The servant therefore fell down before him, saying, "Master, have patience with me, and I will pay you all." Then the master of that servant was moved with compassion, released him, and forgave him the debt.
>
> —MATTHEW 18:25–27

Now let's look at how this parable applies to being offended. When an offense occurs, a debt is owed. You have heard it said, "He'll pay for this." So forgiveness is like the cancellation of a debt.

The king represents God the Father, who forgave

this servant a debt that was impossible for him to pay. In Colossians 2:13–14 we read, "And you, being dead in your trespasses and the uncircumcision of your flesh, He has made alive together with Him, having forgiven you all trespasses, having wiped out the handwriting of [*certificate of debt* with its] requirements that was against us, which was contrary to us. And He has taken it out of the way, having nailed it to the cross."[1]

The debt we were forgiven was unpayable. There was no way we could ever repay God what we owed Him. Our offense was overwhelming. So God gave salvation as a gift. Jesus paid the certificate of debt that was against us. We can see the parallel between this servant's relationship to his king and our relationship with God.

> But that servant went out and found one of his fellow servants who owed him a hundred denarii; and he laid hands on him and took him by the throat, saying, "Pay me what you owe!"
>
> —MATTHEW 18:28

A *denarius* was approximately equal to a laborer's daily wage.[2] So at today's wages one hundred denarii would be worth about four thousand dollars. Now let's continue reading:

> So his fellow servant fell down at his feet and begged him, saying, "Have patience with me, and I will pay you all." And he would not, but went and threw him into prison till he should pay the debt.
> —Matthew 18:29–30

One of his fellow servants owed him a sizable sum of money—one-third of a year's wages. How would you like it if you were missing a third of your salary? But remember that this man was forgiven a debt of 3.2 billion dollars. That's more money than he could earn in a lifetime!

There was no way we could ever repay God what we owed Him.

The offenses we hold against each other compared to our offenses against God are like 4,000 dollars compared to 3.2 billion dollars. We may have been treated badly by someone else, but it does not compare with our transgressions against God.

You may feel no one has it as bad as you do. But you don't realize how badly Jesus was treated. He was innocent, a blameless lamb that was slain.

A person who cannot forgive has forgotten the great debt for which he or she was forgiven. When you realize that Jesus delivered you from eternal death and torment, you will release others unconditionally.

There is nothing worse than eternity in a lake of fire. There is no relief, the worm does not die, and the fire is not quenched. That was our destination until God forgave us through the death of His Son, Jesus Christ. Hallelujah! If you have a hard time forgiving, think of the reality of hell and the love of God that saved you from it.

Lessons for Believers

Let's continue the parable:

> So when his fellow servants saw what had been done, they were very grieved, and came and told their master all that had been done. Then his master, after he had called him, said

to him, "You wicked servant! I forgave you all that debt because you begged me. Should you not also have had compassion on your fellow servant, just as I had pity on you?"

—Matthew 18:31–33

Jesus was not referring to unbelievers in this parable. He was talking about servants of the king. This man already had a great debt forgiven (salvation) and was called the master's "servant." The one he would not forgive was a "fellow servant." So we can conclude that this is the fate of a believer who refuses to forgive.

And his master was angry, and delivered him to the torturers until he should pay all that was due to him. So My heavenly Father also will do to you if each of you, from his heart, does not forgive his brother his trespasses.

—Matthew 18:34–35

These verses have three major points.

1. The unforgiving servant is turned over to torture.
2. He has to pay off the original debt: 375 tons of gold.
3. God the Father will do the same to

any believer who does not forgive a brother's offense.

1. The unforgiving servant is turned over to torture.

Webster's dictionary defines *torture* as "agony of body or mind" or "the infliction of intense pain to punish, coerce or afford sadistic pleasure."

The instigators of this torture are demon spirits. God gives the "torturers" permission to inflict at will pain and agony of body and mind even if we are believers. I have often prayed for people in services who could not receive healing, comfort or deliverance because they would not release others and forgive from their hearts.

> If you have a hard time forgiving, think of the reality of hell and the love of God that saved you from it.

Medical doctors and scientists have linked unforgiveness and bitterness with certain diseases such as arthritis and cancer. Many cases of mental sickness are tied to bitter unforgiveness.

Forgiveness is usually denied to other people, but sometimes it is denied to oneself. Jesus said, "If you have anything against anyone, forgive…" (See Matthew 5:23–24.) *Anyone* includes yourself! If God forgave you, who are you not to forgive one He has forgiven, even if it is you?

2. The unforgiving servant had to pay the original unpayable debt.

He was required to do the impossible. It is like our being required to pay the debt Jesus paid at Calvary. We would lose our salvation.

"Wait a minute," you say. "I thought that once a person prayed the sinner's prayer and committed his life to Jesus he could never be lost."

If you believe that, then explain why Peter wrote the following:

> For if, after they have escaped the pollutions
> of the world through the knowledge of the
> Lord and Savior Jesus Christ, they are again
> entangled in them and overcome, the latter
> end is worse for them than the beginning.
> *For it would have been better for them not to*

have known the way of righteousness, than
having known it, to turn from the holy
commandment delivered to them.
—2 Peter 2:20–21, emphasis added

Peter was talking about people who had
escaped sin ("pollutions of the world") through
salvation in Jesus Christ. However, they were again
entangled by sin (which could be unforgiveness)
and overcome by it. To be overcome meant they
did not return to the Lord and repent of their will-
ful sin. Peter stated that turning from righteousness was worse than never knowing it at all. In
other words, God is saying it is better never to have
gotten saved than to receive the gift of eternal life
and then turn from it permanently.

Jude also described people in the church who
were "twice dead" (Jude 12–13). To be twice dead
means you were once dead without Christ, then you
were made alive by receiving Him, then you died
again by departing from His ways permanently.

We see that many will come to Jesus justifying
themselves by saying, "'Lord, Lord, have we not
prophesied in Your name, cast out demons in Your
name, and done many wonders in Your name?'

And then I will declare to them, 'I never knew you; depart from Me, you who practice lawlessness!'" (Matt. 7:22–23). They knew Him. They called Him Lord and did miracles in His name. But He did not know them.

Whom will Jesus know? The apostle Paul wrote, "But if anyone loves God, this one is known by Him" (1 Cor. 8:3). God knows those who love Him.

You may say, "I love God. I just don't love this brother who has hurt me." Then you are deceived and do not love God, for it is written, "If someone says, 'I love God,' and hates his brother…whom he has seen, how can he love God whom he has not seen?" (1 John 4:20). Deception is a terrible thing, for the deceived believes with all of his heart that he is right. He believes he is one way when he is really another. A person who refuses to obey the Word deceives his own heart.

Isn't it interesting that "many" will expect to enter heaven and be refused? Jesus said many would be offended in the last days (Matt. 24:10). Could these two groups include the same people?

Some believers are so tormented by unforgiveness that they may hope death will bring relief. But this is not true. We must deal with unforgiveness now or be called upon to pay the unpayable.

3. God the Father will do this to any believer who refuses to forgive from the heart—no matter how great the hurt or offense.

Jesus was very specific, making sure we understood this parable. In almost every parable Jesus did not offer the interpretation unless His disciples asked for it. In this case, however, He wanted no question about the severity of judgment for those who refused to forgive.

> A person who refuses
> to obey the Word
> deceives his own heart.

In many other instances Jesus also made it clear that if we would not forgive we would not be forgiven. Remember that He is not like us—He means what He says.

Many times in the church, excuses are given for harboring unforgiveness. Unforgiveness is considered to be a lesser sin than homosexuality, adultery, theft, drunkenness and so on. But those who practice it will not inherit the kingdom of God—just as those who practice other sins will not inherit God's kingdom.

Some may think this is a hard message, but I see it as a message of mercy and warning, not of harsh judgment. Would you rather be convicted by the Holy Spirit now and experience genuine repentance and forgiveness? Or would you rather refuse to forgive until you can no longer repent, and then hear the Master say, "Depart"?

Adapted from *The Bait of Satan*, 134–141.

THREE

The Trap
of Revenge

DEVELOPING
Inner Strength

I was ministering on the subject of offenses at a church in Tampa, Florida. Afterward a woman came to me. She said she had forgiven her ex-husband for all he'd done. But as she listened to me talk about releasing offenses, she realized she still did not have peace inside and was very uncomfortable.

"You still have not forgiven him," I told her gently.

"Yes, I have," she said. "I have cried tears of forgiveness."

"You may have cried, but you still have not released him."

She insisted that I was wrong and that she had forgiven him. "I don't want anything from him. I have released him."

"Tell me what he did to you," I said.

"My husband and I pastored a church. He left me and our three boys and ran away with a prominent woman in the church." Tears formed in her eyes. "He said he'd missed God by marrying me because it was God's perfect will for him to marry the woman with whom he ran away. He told me she was an asset to his ministry because she was much more supportive. He said I was a hindrance. He said I was critical. He put all the blame of the marriage breakup on me. He has never come back and admitted that any of it was his fault."

This man was obviously deceived and had greatly wronged his wife and family. She had suffered much from his actions and was waiting for him to pay back a debt. The debt was not alimony or child support, for her new husband was providing all this for her. The debt she wanted him to pay was to admit that he had been wrong and that she had been right.

"You won't forgive him until he comes to you and says that he was wrong, that it was his fault, not yours, and then asks for your forgiveness. This is the unfulfilled payment that has kept you bound," I pointed out to her.

Holding on to an offense of unforgiveness is like holding a debt against someone. When one person is wronged by another, he believes that a debt is owed to him. He expects a payment of some sort, whether monetary or not.

Our court system exists to avenge wronged or injured parties. Lawsuits result from people trying to satisfy their debts. When a person has been hurt by another, human justice says, "They will stand trial for what they have done and pay if found guilty." The unforgiving servant wanted his fellow servant to pay what he owed, so he sought his compensation in the court of law. This is not the way of righteousness.

> Beloved, do not avenge yourselves, but rather give place to wrath; for it is written, "Vengeance is Mine, I will repay," says the Lord.
>
> —Romans 12:19

It is unrighteous for us as children of God to avenge ourselves. But that is exactly what we are seeking when we refuse to forgive. We desire, seek, plan and carry out revenge. We will not forgive until the debt is paid in full, and only we can determine the acceptable compensation. When we seek to correct the wrong done to us, we set ourselves up as judges. But we know:

> There is one Lawgiver, who is able to save and to destroy. Who are you to judge another?...Do not grumble against one another, brethren, lest you be condemned. Behold, the Judge is standing at the door!
> —James 4:12; 5:9

God is the just Judge. He will pass righteous judgment. But He will repay according to righteousness. If someone has done wrong and genuinely repents, Jesus' work at Calvary erases the debt.

You may say, "But the wrong was done to me, not to Jesus!"

It is unrighteous for us as children of God to avenge ourselves.

Yes, but you don't realize the wrong you did to

Him. An innocent victim, He bore no guilt while every other human had sinned and was condemned to die. Each one of us has broken laws of God that transcend the laws of the land. All of us should be condemned to death by the hand of the highest court in the universe if justice is served.

You may have done nothing to provoke the wrong you incurred at the hand of another. But if you contrast what was done to you with what you've been forgiven of, there is no comparison. It would not even put a dent in the debt you owe! If you feel cheated, you have lost your concept of the mercy extended you.

No Gray Grudge Areas

Under the Old Testament covenant, if you trespassed against me, I had legal rights to bring the same back on you. Permission was granted to collect on debts, repaying evil for evil. (See Leviticus 24:19; Exodus 21:23–25.) Law was supreme. Jesus had not yet died to set them free.

Look how He addresses New Covenant believers.

> *You have heard that it was said,* "An eye for an eye and a tooth for a tooth." *But I tell you*

not to resist an evil person. But whoever slaps you on your right cheek, turn the other to him also. If anyone wants to sue you and take away your tunic, let him have your cloak also. And whoever compels you to go one mile, go with him two. Give to him who asks you, and from him who wants to borrow from you do not turn away.

—MATTHEW 5:38–42, EMPHASIS ADDED

Jesus eliminates any gray areas for grudges. In fact, He says that our attitude is to be so far removed from avenging ourselves that we are willing to open ourselves to the possibility of being taken advantage of again.

When we seek to correct the wrong done to us we set ourselves up as a judge. The unforgiving servant in Matthew 18 did this when he put his fellow servant in jail. In turn, this unforgiving servant was turned over to the tormentors and his family sold until he should pay all.

If Jesus had waited for us to come to Him and apologize, saying, "We were wrong. You were right. Forgive us," He would *not* have forgiven us from the cross. As He hung on the cross, He cried out, "Father, forgive them, for they do not know what they do" (Luke 23:34). He forgave us before we came to Him confessing our offense against Him. We are admonished by the words of the apostle Paul: "Even as Christ forgave you, so you also must do" (Col. 3:13). In another verse, Paul admonishes, "Be kind to one another, tenderhearted, forgiving one another, even as God in Christ forgave you" (Eph. 4:32).

> When we seek to correct
> the wrong done to us we set
> ourselves up as a judge.

When I told the woman with whom I spoke in Tampa, Florida, "You won't forgive him until he says, 'I was wrong—you were right,'" tears streamed down her face. What she wanted seemed small in comparison to all the pain he had brought to her and her children. But she was in bondage to human justice. She had set herself up as a judge, claiming her right to the debt and waiting for payment. This offense had hindered her relationship with her new husband. It had also affected her relationship with all male authorities because her former husband had been her pastor as well.

Often Jesus likened the condition of our hearts to that of soil. We are admonished to be rooted and grounded in the love of God. The seed of God's Word will then take root in our hearts and grow and eventually produce the fruit of righteousness. This fruit is love, joy, peace, longsuffering, kindness, goodness, faithfulness, gentleness and self-control (Gal. 5:22–23).

The ground will produce only what is planted in it. If we plant seeds of debt, unforgiveness and offense, another root will spring up in place of the love of God. It is called the root of bitterness.

Francis Frangipane gave an excellent definition of bitterness: "Bitterness is unfulfilled revenge."[1] It is produced when revenge is not satisfied to the degree we desire.

The writer of the Book of Hebrews spoke directly about this issue.

> Pursue peace with all people, and holiness, without which no one will see the Lord: looking carefully lest anyone fall short of the grace of God; lest any *root of bitterness*

> springing up cause trouble, and by this
> *many become defiled.*
> > —HEBREWS 12:14–15, EMPHASIS ADDED

Notice the words "many become defiled." Could this again be the "many" Jesus said would be offended in the last days? (See Matthew 24:10.)

Bitterness is a root. If roots are nursed—watered, protected, fed and given attention—they increase in depth and strength. If not dealt with quickly, roots are hard to pull up. The strength of the offense will continue to grow. We are exhorted not to let the sun go down on our wrath (Eph. 4:26). If we do not deal quickly with our wrath, instead of the fruit of righteousness being produced, we will see a harvest of anger, resentment, jealousy, hatred, strife and discord. Jesus called these evil fruits. (See Matthew 7:19–20.)

The Bible says a person who does not pursue peace by releasing offenses will eventually become defiled. That which is precious will end up being corrupted by the vileness of unforgiveness.

A Potential King Defiled

After the death of King Saul, David ascended to

the throne. He strengthened the nation, enjoyed military and financial success and held the throne securely. His children included Amnon, his oldest son, and Absalom, his third-born son.

David's son Amnon committed a wicked offense against his half sister Tamar, who was Absalom's sister. Amnon pretended to be ill and asked his father to send Tamar to serve him food. When she did, he ordered the servants out and raped her. He then despised her and had her removed from his sight. He had disgraced a virgin royal princess, devastating her life with shame. (See 2 Samuel 13.)

Without saying a word to his half brother, Absalom brought his sister into his own home and provided for her. But he hated Amnon for defiling Tamar.

Absalom expected his father to punish his half brother. King David was outraged when he heard of Amnon's wickedness, but he took no course of action. Absalom was devastated by his father's lack of justice.

Tamar had once worn the royal robes reserved for the king's virgin daughters; now she was robed in shame. She was a beautiful girl and had probably been held in high esteem by the people. Now she lived in seclusion, unable to marry because she was no longer a virgin.

It was unfair. She had attended Amnon at the king's command, and she was raped. Her life was over, while the man who committed this atrocity lived as if nothing had happened. She bore the weight of it all, her life in shambles.

Day after day Absalom saw his grieving sister. The perfect existence of a princess had become a nightmare. Absalom waited a year for his father to do something, but David did nothing. Absalom was offended by his father's nonresponse, and he hated the wicked Amnon.

After two years his hatred for Amnon birthed a plot to murder him. Absalom probably thought, *I will avenge my sister since the proper authority chooses to do nothing.*

He threw a feast for all the king's sons. When Amnon did not suspect him, Absalom had him killed. Absalom then fled to Geshur, his revenge accomplished against Amnon. But the offense he carried against his father burned stronger, especially while he was away from the palace.

Absalom's thoughts were poisoned with bitterness. He became an expert critic of David's weaknesses. Yet he hoped his father would call for him. David did not. This fueled Absalom's resentment.

Perhaps these were his thoughts: *My father is hailed by the people, but they are blind to his true nature. He is only a self-seeking man who uses God as a cover-up. Why, he is worse than King Saul! Saul lost his throne for not killing the king of the Amalekites and for sparing a few of their best sheep and oxen. My father has committed adultery with the wife of one of his most loyal men. Then he covered his sin by killing the man who was loyal to him. He is a murderer and an adulterer—that is why he did not punish Amnon! And he covers all this up with his fake worship of Jehovah.*

Absalom stayed in Geshur for three years. David had been comforted over the death of his son Amnon, and Joab had convinced the king to bring Absalom home. But David still refused to meet Absalom face to face. Two more years went by, and David finally returned Absalom to favor and granted him full privileges again. But the offense in Absalom's heart stayed just as strong.

Absalom was an expert in appearances. Before he murdered Amnon, "Absalom spoke to his brother Amnon neither good nor bad. For Absalom hated Amnon" (2 Sam. 13:22). Many people are able to hide their offense and hatred as Absalom did.

Out of this offended critical attitude, he began to draw to himself anyone who was discontented. He made himself available to all Israel, taking time to listen to their complaints. He would lament that things would be different if only he were king. He judged their cases since it appeared the king had no time for them. Perhaps Absalom judged their cases because he felt he had not been served justice in his own.

He seemed to be concerned for the people. The Bible says Absalom stole the hearts of Israel from his father, David. But was he genuinely concerned for them, or was he seeking a way to overthrow David, the one who had offended him?

Experts on Error

Absalom drew Israel to him and rose up against David. King David had to flee Jerusalem for his life. It looked as if Absalom would establish his own kingdom. Instead, he was killed as he pursued David, even though David had ordered that he remain untouched.

> # The root of bitterness is barely noticeable as it develops.

Absalom was, in fact, killed by his own bitterness and offense. The man with so much potential, heir to the throne, died in his prime because he refused to release the debt he thought his father owed. He ended up defiled.

Assistants to leaders in a church often become offended by the person they serve. As a result, they soon become critical—experts at all that is wrong with their leader or those he or she appoints. They become offended. Their sight is distorted. They see from a totally different perspective from God's.

They believe their mission in life is to deliver those around them from an unfair leader. They win the hearts of the disgruntled, discontented and ignorant, and before they know it they end up splitting or dividing the church or ministry—just as Absalom did.

Sometimes their observations are correct. Perhaps David *should have* taken action against Amnon. Perhaps a leader does have areas of error. Who is the judge—you or the Lord? Remember that if you sow strife, you will reap it.

What happened to Absalom, as well as what happens in modern ministries, is a process that takes time. We are often unaware that an offense has entered our hearts. The root of bitterness is barely noticeable as it develops. But as it is nursed it will grow and be strengthened. As the writer of Hebrews exhorts, we are to look "carefully…lest any root of bitterness springing up cause trouble, and by this many become defiled" (Heb. 12:15).

We must examine our hearts and open ourselves to the correction of the Lord, for only His Word can discern the thoughts and intentions of our hearts. The Holy Spirit convicts as He speaks through one's conscience. We must not ignore His conviction or quench Him. If you have done this, repent before God, and open your heart to His correction.

A minister once asked me if he had acted as an Absalom or a David in something he had done. He had served as an assistant to a pastor in a city, and the pastor fired him. It seemed that the senior pastor was jealous and afraid of this young man because God's hand was on him.

A year later, the minister who was fired believed the Lord wanted him to start a church on the other side of the city. So he did, and some of the people from the church he had left came over to join him. He was troubled because he did not want to act as an Absalom. Apparently he did not harbor an offense from his former leader. He started the new church at the leading of the Lord—not as a response to the lack of care at the other church.

I pointed out to him the difference between Absalom and David. Absalom stole the hearts of others because he was offended with his leader. David encouraged others to stay loyal to Saul even though Saul was attacking him. Absalom took men with him; David left alone.

"Did you leave your church alone?" I asked him. "Did you do anything to encourage people to come with you or to support you?"

"I left alone and did nothing to draw people with me," he said.

"That's fine. You have acted as a David. Make sure the people who come to you are not offended with your former pastor. If they are, lead them to freedom and healing."

Do not be afraid to allow the Holy Spirit to reveal any unforgiveness or bitterness.

This man's church is now prospering. What I appreciated so much about him was that he was not afraid to examine his own heart. Not only that, but he submitted himself to godly counsel. It was more important to him that he was submitted to God's way than that he was proven "right."

Do not be afraid to allow the Holy Spirit to reveal any unforgiveness or bitterness. The longer you hide it, the stronger it will become and the harder your heart will grow. Stay tenderhearted. How?

Let all bitterness, wrath, anger, clamor, and

evil speaking be put away from you, with all malice. And be kind to one another, tenderhearted, forgiving one another, even as God in Christ forgave you.

—Ephesians 4:31–32

Adapted from *The Bait of Satan*, 143–152.

FOUR

Seeking Reconciliation

DEVELOPING
Inner Strength

There are limitless scenarios for offense. Maybe the person we have offended believes we were unjust in our treatment of him, when in reality we did him no harm. He may have inaccurate information, which has yielded an inaccurate conclusion.

On the other hand, he may have accurate information from which he has drawn an inaccurate conclusion. What we said may have been grossly distorted once it was processed through the various channels of communication. Though our intent was not to harm, our words and actions gave a different appearance.

Often we judge ourselves by our intentions and everyone else by their actions. It is possible to intend one thing while communicating something totally different. Sometimes our true motives are cleverly hidden even from us. We want to believe they are pure. But as we filter them through the

Word of God we see them differently.

Finally, maybe we did sin against the person. We were angry or under pressure, and he got the brunt of it. Or maybe this person has constantly and deliberately lashed out at us, and we were responding in kind.

No matter what caused it, this offended person's understanding is darkened, and he has based his judgments on assumptions, hearsay and appearances, deceiving himself even though he believes he has discerned our true motives. How can we have an accurate judgment without accurate information? We must be sensitive to the fact that he believes with his whole heart that he has been wronged. For whatever reason he feels this way, we must be willing to humble ourselves and apologize.

Jesus is exhorting us to reconcile even if the offense is not our fault. It takes maturity to walk in humility in order to bring reconciliation. But taking the first step is often harder on the one who is hurting. That's why Jesus told the person who caused the offense to "go to him..."

I n the Sermon on the Mount—probably the most important teaching Jesus left us—He said these words:

> You have heard that it was said to those of old, "You shall not murder, and whoever murders will be in danger of the judgment." But I say to you that whoever is angry with his brother without a cause shall be in danger of the judgment. And whoever says to his brother, "Raca!" shall be in danger of the council. But whoever says, "You fool!" shall be in danger of hell fire. Therefore if you bring your gift to the altar, and there remember that your brother has something against you, leave your gift there before the altar, and go your way. First be reconciled to your brother, and then come and offer your gift.
>
> —MATTHEW 5:21–24

This quote comes from the Sermon on the Mount. Jesus started by saying, "You have heard that it was said to those of old…" Then He said, "But I say to you…" Jesus continues this comparison throughout this portion of His message. First He quotes the law that regulates our outward actions. Then He shows its fulfillment by bringing it into the heart.

In God's eyes, a murderer is not limited to the one who commits murder; he is also the one who hates his brother. What you are in your heart is how you really are!

Jesus clearly delineates the consequences of offense in this portion of His sermon. He illustrates the severity of holding anger or bitter offense. If one is angry with his brother without a cause, he is in danger of judgment. He is in danger of the council if that anger bears fruit and he calls his brother "Raca!"[1]

The word *raca* means "empty-headed," or fool. It was a term of reproach used among the Jews in the time of Christ. If that anger reaches the point where a person calls a brother a fool, he is in danger of hell. The word *fool* means to be godless.[2] The fool says in his heart there is no God (Ps. 14:1). In those days, to call a brother a fool was quite a serious accusation. No one would say such a thing unless the anger he bore had turned to hatred. Today it would be comparable to telling a brother, "Go to hell," and meaning it.

Jesus was showing the people that not dealing with anger could lead to hatred. Hatred not dealt with would put them in danger of hell. Then He said that if they remembered their brother was offended with them, they were to make it top priority to find him and seek to be reconciled.

Why should we seek with such urgency to be reconciled—for our sake or for our brother's sake? We should go for his sake that we might be a catalyst to help him out of the offense. Even if we are not offended with him, the love of God does not let him remain angry without attempting to reach out and restore. We may have done nothing wrong. Right or wrong doesn't matter. It is more important for us to help this stumbling brother than to prove ourselves correct.

Asking Forgiveness of One Who Is Offended

The apostle Paul said:

> Therefore let us pursue the things which make for peace and the things by which one may edify another.
>
> —Romans 14:19

This shows us how to approach a person we have offended. If we go with an attitude of frustration we will not promote peace. We will only make it difficult for the one who is hurt. We are to maintain an attitude of pursuing peace through humility at the expense of our pride. It is the only way to see true reconciliation.

On certain occasions I have approached people I have hurt or who were angry with me, and they have lashed out at me. I have been told I was selfish, inconsiderate, proud, rude, harsh and more.

> We are to maintain an attitude of pursuing peace through humility at the expense of our pride.

My natural response has been to say, "No, I'm not. You just don't understand me!" But when I defend myself, it only fuels their fire of offense. This is not pursuing peace. Standing up for "our rights" and ourselves will never bring true peace.

Instead I have learned to listen and keep my mouth shut until they have said what they need to say. If I don't agree, I let them know I respect what they have said and will search my attitude and intentions. Then I tell them I am sorry I have hurt them.

Other times they are accurate in their assessment of me. I admit, "You are right. I ask your forgiveness."

Once again it simply means humbling ourselves to promote reconciliation. Perhaps this was why Jesus said in the next verses:

> Agree with your adversary quickly, while you are on the way with him, lest your adversary deliver you to the judge, the judge hand you over to the officer, and you be thrown into prison. Assuredly, I say to you, you will by no means get out of there till you have paid the last penny.
>
> —MATTHEW 5:25–26

Pride defends. Humility agrees and says, "You are right. I have acted this way. Please forgive me."

> But the wisdom that is from above is first pure, then peaceable, gentle, *willing to yield*, full of mercy and good fruits, without

partiality and without hypocrisy.

—James 3:17, emphasis added

Godly wisdom is willing to yield. It is not stiff-necked or stubborn when it comes to personal conflicts. A person submitted to godly wisdom is not afraid to yield or defer to the other person's viewpoint as long as it does not violate truth.

Approaching Someone Who Has Offended You

Now that we have discussed what to do when we offend our brother, let's consider what to do if our brother offends us.

> Moreover if your brother sins against you, go and tell him his fault between you and him alone. If he hears you, you have gained your brother.
>
> —Matthew 18:15

Many people apply this Scripture verse in a different attitude from the one Jesus was intending. If they have been hurt, they will go and confront the offender in a spirit of revenge and anger. They use this verse as justification to condemn the one who has hurt them.

But they are missing the whole reason Jesus instructed us to go to one another. It is not for condemnation but for reconciliation. He does not want us to tell our brother how rotten he has been to us. We are to go to remove the breach preventing the restoration of our relationship.

This parallels how God restores us to Himself. We have sinned against God, but He "demonstrates His own love toward [and for] us, in that while we were still sinners, Christ died for us" (Rom. 5:8). Are we willing to lay down our self-protection and die to pride in order to be restored to the one who has offended us? God reached out to us before we asked for forgiveness. Jesus decided to forgive us before we even acknowledged our offense.

Even though He reached out to us, we could not be reconciled to the Father until we received His word of reconciliation.

> Now all things are of God, who has *reconciled* us to Himself through Jesus Christ, and has given us the ministry of *reconciliation,* that is, that God was in Christ reconciling the world to Himself, not imputing their trespasses to them, and has committed to us the *word of reconciliation.* Now then,

we are ambassadors for Christ, as though
God were pleading through us: *we implore
you on Christ's behalf, be reconciled to God.*
—2 CORINTHIANS 5:18–20, EMPHASIS ADDED

The work of reconciliation begins on the common ground that we all have sinned against God. We do not desire reconciliation or salvation unless we know there is a separation.

In the New Testament, the disciples preached that the people had sinned against God. But why tell people they have sinned? To condemn them? God does not condemn. "For God did not send His Son into the world to condemn the world, but that the world through Him might be saved" (John 3:17). Is it rather to bring them to a place where they realize their condition, repent of their sins and ask forgiveness?

What leads men to repentance? The answer is found in Romans 2:4:

Or do you despise the riches of His goodness, forbearance, and longsuffering, not knowing that the goodness of God leads you to repentance?

God's goodness leads us to repent. His love does

not leave us condemned to hell. He proved His love by sending Jesus, His only Son, to the cross to die for us. God reaches out first, even though we have sinned against Him. He reaches out not to condemn but to restore—to save.

Since we are to imitate God, we are to extend reconciliation to a brother who sins against us. Jesus established this pattern: Go to him and show him his sin, not to condemn him but to remove anything that lies between the two of you. Then you can be reconciled and restored. The goodness of God within us will draw our brother to repentance and restoration of the relationship.

> I, therefore, the prisoner of the Lord, beseech you to walk worthy of the calling with which you were called, with all lowliness and gentleness, with longsuffering, bearing with one another in love, endeavoring to keep the unity of the Spirit in the bond of peace.
> —EPHESIANS 4:1–3

We keep this bond of peace by maintaining an attitude of humility, gentleness and longsuffering and by undergirding each other's weakness in love. The bonds of love are strengthened thereby.

I have wronged people who have confronted me with condemnation. As a result I lost all desire to be reconciled. In fact, I thought they didn't want reconciliation—they just wanted me to know they were mad.

Others I have wronged have come to me in meekness. Then I was quick to change my outlook and ask forgiveness—sometimes before they had finished speaking.

> We should not go to a brother who has offended us until we have decided to forgive him from our hearts.

Has someone ever come to you and said, "I just want you to know that I forgive you for not being a better friend and for not doing this or that for me"?

Then when they have blasted you, they give you a look that says, "You owe me an apology."

You are baffled and stand there in confusion and hurt. They did not come to reconcile your relationship but to intimidate and control you.

We should not go to a brother who has offended us until we have decided to forgive him from our hearts—no matter how he responds to us. We need to get rid of any feelings of animosity toward him before approaching him. If we don't, we will probably react out of these negative feelings and hurt him, not heal him.

What happens if we have the right attitude and attempt to reconcile with someone who has sinned against us, but he or she won't listen?

> But if he will not hear, take with you one or two more, that "by the mouth of two or three witnesses every word may be established." And if he refuses to hear them, tell it to the church. But if he refuses even to hear the church, let him be to you like a heathen and a tax collector.
>
> —Matthew 18:16–17

Each of these progressions has the same goal—reconciliation. In essence Jesus was saying, "Keep trying." Notice how the one who caused the offense is involved at every step. How often we take offenses to everyone else before we go to the one who sinned against us, as Jesus told us to do! We do this because we have not dealt with our own hearts. We feel justified as we tell everyone our side of the story. It strengthens our cause and comforts us when others agree with how badly we have been treated. There is only selfishness in this type of behavior.

The Bottom Line

If we keep the love of God as our motivation, we will not fail. Love never fails. When we love others the way Jesus loves us, we will be free even if the other person chooses not to be reconciled to us. Look carefully at the following Scripture verse. God's wisdom is available for all situations.

> If it is possible, as much as depends on you,
> live peaceably with all men.
>
> —ROMANS 12:18

Paul says "If it is possible…" because there are times when others will refuse to be at peace with us. There may be those whose conditions for reconciliation would compromise our relationship with the Lord. In either case it is not possible to restore that relationship.

Notice that he continues, "...as much as depends on you." We are to do everything we can to be reconciled with the other person, as long as we remain loyal to truth. We often give up relationships too soon.

> ## If we keep the love of God as our motivation, we will not fail.

I will never forget the time when a friend counseled me not to walk away from a very frustrating situation. "John, I know you can find scriptural reasons for walking away. But before you do that, make sure you have fought this in prayer and done all you can to bring the peace of God into this situation."

Then he added, "You will regret it if you look back one day and ask yourself if you did all you could to save this relationship. It is better to know that you have no other recourse and that you did as much as possible without compromising truth."

I was very grateful for his counsel and recognized it as the wisdom of God.

Remember Jesus' words:

> Blessed are the peacemakers, for they shall
> be called sons of God.
>
> —MATTHEW 5:9

He did not say, "Blessed are the peacekeepers." A peacekeeper avoids confrontation at all costs to maintain peace, even at the risk of compromising truth. But the peace he maintains is not true peace. It is a touchy, superficial peace that will not last.

A peacemaker will go in love and confront, bringing truth so that the resulting reconciliation will endure. He will not maintain an artificial, superficial relationship. He desires openness, truth and love. He refuses to hide offense with a political smile. He makes peace with a bold love that cannot fail.

God is this way with mankind. He is not willing that any should perish. But He will not compromise truth for a relationship. He seeks reconciliation with true commitment, not on superficial terms. This develops a bond of love that no evil can sever. He has laid His life down for us. We can only do likewise.

The love of God is the key to freedom from the baited trap of offense.

Remember that the bottom line is the love of God. It never fails, never fades and never comes to an end. It seeks not its own. It is not easily offended (1 Cor. 13:5).

The apostle Paul wrote that love would overcome all kinds of sin.

> And this I pray, that *your love may abound still more and more* in knowledge and all discernment, that you may approve the things that are excellent, that you may be sincere and *without offense* till the day of Christ, being filled with the fruits of righteousness which are by Jesus Christ, to the glory and praise of God.
> —Philippians 1:9–11, emphasis added

The love of God is the key to freedom from the baited trap of offense. This must be an abounding love, a love that continually grows and is strengthened in our hearts.

So many in our society today are deceived by a superficial love, a love that talks but does not act. The love that will keep us from stumbling lays down its life selflessly—even for the good of an enemy. When we walk in this kind of love, we cannot be seduced into taking the bait of Satan.

Adapted from *The Bait of Satan*, 165–174.

FIVE

Set Others Free

DEVELOPING
Inner Strength

On my second ministry trip to Indonesia I took Lisa, my children and a babysitter. We arrived in Denpasar, Bali, a resort island.

An elder in the church we were visiting owned a modest hotel in a very noisy section of town. We had traveled a long distance and had had very little sleep. We were exhausted. That night we were awakened several times by loud noises and barking dogs. We only stayed overnight and did not get the rest we needed.

The following day we continued on to Java and ministered for the next two weeks on a very busy schedule. We had only one free day in that two weeks, and that was for travel. In one twenty-four-hour period we ministered five times at a church with thirty thousand members.

At the end of the trip we were scheduled to go back through Bali. The pastor informed us that we would be staying at his elder's hotel again. We were not thrilled about being in those conditions again after two solid weeks of ministry.

At breakfast on the morning we were to leave Java for Bali, a precious lady offered to pay for our accommodations at one of the finest resort hotels in Bali. I was so excited because we would get to rest and stay in a beautiful place.

As we left the restaurant to pack, Lisa told me she did not feel good about accepting this lady's offer. The interpreter and I reasoned with her and said it would be fine. Again on the plane from Java to Bali, she said she didn't think we were doing the right thing.

I was foolish and didn't listen to her. I told her it wouldn't cost the church anything and it would be fine. When we arrived in Bali, she pleaded with me at the baggage claim one more time, but I ignored her.

When we met the pastor, I told him we would not need to stay at the elder's hotel because of the woman's offer. He seemed uneasy with what I had said, so I asked him what was wrong.

Fortunately he was open with me and said, "John, this will offend the elder and his family. They've already reserved the room for you, and they're sold out for the evening."

I had also apparently offended the pastor because I did not appreciate what they had arranged for us. Finally I told him we would stay at the elder's hotel and pass up the woman's offer.

The Lord dealt with me about my attitude. I knew the pastor was hurt. I saw that demanding my rights had offended this brother and that it was a sin. I asked for his forgiveness. He forgave me. I hope I don't have to learn that lesson again.

We have learned that Jesus offended many as He traveled and ministered. It appears that almost everywhere He went people were offended. However, in this chapter I want to look at the flip side of this— a time when Jesus could easily have been offended by something that happened to Him.

Jesus and His disciples had just returned to Capernaum. They had completed a ministry circuit and had come for a short, but much needed, rest. If there was any place that could be considered a base for His ministry, it was this city.

While there, Simon Peter was approached by the official in charge of collecting the temple tax. The official asked, "Does your Teacher not pay the temple tax?" (Matt. 17:24).

Peter answered yes and went back to discuss it with Jesus.

Jesus anticipated the tax collector's request, so He inquired of Simon Peter, "What do you think, Simon? From whom do the kings of the earth take customs or taxes, from their sons or from strangers?"

"From strangers," Peter told Him.

"Then the sons are free," Jesus responded (Matt. 17:25–26).

Jesus was making a point with Peter that "sons are free." They are not the ones who supply the taxes—they are the ones who enjoy the benefits of the tax. They live in the palace maintained by taxes. The sons eat at the king's table and wear royal apparel, all provided by the tax. They are free and freely provided for.

This official received the temple tax. But who was king or owner of the temple? In whose honor was it built? Of course, the answer was God the Father.

Jesus asked Peter this question just after Peter had received the revelation from God that Jesus was "the Christ, *the Son* of the living God." In essence, Jesus was asking Peter, "If I am the Son of the One who owns the temple, then am I not free from paying temple tax?" Of course He would be exempt. Jesus would be totally justified in not paying the tax. Yet watch what He says to Simon Peter:

> *Nevertheless, lest we offend them,* go to the sea, cast in a hook, and take the fish that comes up first. And when you have opened

> its mouth, you will find a piece of money;
> take that and give it to them for Me and you.
>   —MATTHEW 17:27, EMPHASIS ADDED

He had just proven His liberty. But in order not to offend He said to Peter, "Let's pay it!" It was yet another confirmation of His freedom when He instructed Peter to go and fish and take the first fish that came up; in its mouth he would find money. God the Father even provided the tax money.

Jesus is Lord of the earth. He is the Son of God. The earth and everything in it are created by Him and are subject to Him. Therefore, He knew the money would be in that fish's mouth. He did not have to work for that money because He was the Son. And yet He still chose to pay the tax and not to offend.

Jesus chose to use His liberty and freedom to serve.

Is this the same Jesus who offended people and made no apologies for it? He proved He was exempt from the temple tax, but said, "Lest we offend them, go and pay it!" It seems as if there is some inconsistency—or is there? Our answer is found in the next verse.

> At that time the disciples came to Jesus, saying, "Who then is greatest in the kingdom of heaven?" Then Jesus called a little child to Him, set him in the midst of them, and said, "Assuredly, I say to you, unless you are converted and become as little children, you will by no means enter the kingdom of heaven. Therefore whoever humbles himself as this little child is the greatest in the kingdom of heaven."
>
> —MATTHEW 18:1–4

The key phrase here is "whoever humbles himself." A little later Jesus amplified this by saying:

> Whoever desires to become great among you, let him be your servant…just as the Son of Man did not come to be served, but to serve, and to give His life a ransom for many.
>
> —MATTHEW 20:26–28

Wow! What a statement! He did not come to be served but to serve. He was the Son; He was free; He owed no one anything; He was subject to no man. Yet He chose to use His liberty and freedom to serve.

Liberated to Serve

We are exhorted in the New Testament as sons of God to imitate Christ, to have the same attitude we see in Jesus.

> For you, brethren, have been called to liberty; only do not use liberty as an opportunity for the flesh, but through love serve one another.
>
> —GALATIANS 5:13

Another word for liberty is *privilege*. We are not to use our liberty or privileges as children of the living God to serve ourselves. Liberty is to be used to serve others. There is freedom in serving but bondage in slavery. A slave is one who *has* to serve while a servant is one who *lives* to serve. Let's look at some of the differences between a slave's attitude and a servant's:

- A *slave* has to—a *servant* gets to.
- A *slave* does the minimum requirement—a *servant* reaches the maximum potential.

- A *slave* goes one mile—a *servant* goes the extra mile.
- A *slave* feels robbed—a *servant* gives.
- A *slave* is bound—a *servant* is free.
- A *slave* fights for his rights—a *servant* lays down his rights.

I have seen many Christians serve with a resentful attitude. They give grudgingly and complain as they pay their taxes. They still live as slaves to a law from which they have been set free. They remain slaves in their hearts. They do not have the "spirit" in which Jesus gave His commands. They have not realized they were liberated to serve. So they continue to fight for their own benefit rather than for the benefit of others.

> A slave is one who has to
> serve while a servant is
> one who lives to serve.

Paul gives a vivid example of confronting this attitude in his letters to the Romans and the

Corinthians. Liberty for these believers was challenged by issues about food. Paul began by exhorting them to "receive one who is weak in the faith, but not to disputes over doubtful things. For one believes he may eat all things, but he who is weak eats only vegetables" (Rom. 14:1–2).

Jesus had clarified that it was not what goes into the mouth that defiles but what comes out of the mouth. When He made this statement, He made all foods clean to the believer (Mark 7:18–19).

Paul said that there were some believers who were weak in their faith and still could not eat meat for fear of eating food that had been sacrificed to idols. Though Jesus had spoken to the issue, these people still could not eat meat with a clear conscience.

> Therefore concerning the eating of things offered to idols, we know that an idol is nothing in the world…yet for us there is one God, the Father, of whom are all things, and we for Him; and one Lord Jesus Christ, through whom are all things, and through whom we live. However, there is not in everyone that knowledge; for some, with consciousness of the idol, until now eat it as a thing offered to an idol; and their

conscience, being weak, is defiled.

—1 Corinthians 8:4, 6–7

In those churches Christians with stronger faith were eating meats of questionable origin in front of weaker saints. This was causing a problem even though Jesus had purified these foods. The weaker ones could not shake the image of the meat on the altar of an idol. The stronger saints knew that an idol was nothing and felt no prick of conscience as they ate.

But it appears that they were more concerned with holding on to their rights as New Testament believers than they were with offending their brethren. Without realizing it they had placed a stumbling block in the path of their weaker brothers. This attitude is not present in the heart of a servant. Look how Paul addressed them:

> Therefore let us not judge one another any-more, but rather resolve this, not to put a stumbling block or a cause to fall in our brother's way…for the kingdom of God is not eating and drinking, but righteousness and peace and joy in the Holy Spirit.
>
> —Romans 14:13, 17

He was saying, "Let's remember what the kingdom is really about—righteousness, peace and joy in the Holy Spirit." All of these benefits were being upset in the new believers. The stronger believers were not using their liberty to serve but as a platform for their "rights." They had knowledge of their New Testament freedom. But knowledge without love destroys.

They did not have the heart of Jesus in this matter. Jesus proved His rights regarding the temple tax to Peter and the rest of the disciples to exemplify the importance of laying down our lives to serve. He never wanted freedom to be a license to demand our rights and cause another to be offended and stumble.

Paul gave this warning to those who had knowledge of their rights in Christ without His heart to serve.

> And because of your knowledge shall the weak brother perish, for whom Christ died? But when you thus sin against the brethren, and wound their weak conscience, you sin against Christ.
>
> —1 CORINTHIANS 8:11–12

We can use our liberty to sin. How? By wounding those of weaker conscience, causing one of Christ's little ones to be offended and stumble.

Laying Down Our Rights

After Jesus established His liberty in reference to the temple tax, He was careful to charge His disciples with the importance of humility.

> Whoever causes one of these little ones who believe in Me to sin, it would be better for him if a millstone were hung around his neck, and he were drowned in the depth of the sea. Woe to the world because of offenses! For offenses must come, but woe to that man by whom the offense comes!
>
> If your hand or foot causes you to sin, cut it off and cast it from you. It is better for you to enter into life lame or maimed, rather than having two hands or two feet, to be cast into the everlasting fire. And if your eye causes you to sin, pluck it out and cast it from you. It is better for you to enter into life with one eye, rather than having two eyes, to be cast into hell fire.
>
> Take heed that you do not despise one of

these little ones, for I say to you that in heaven their angels always see the face of My Father who is in heaven.

—MATTHEW 18:6–10

This entire chapter of Matthew is about offenses. Jesus is clearly saying to get rid of whatever causes sin, even if it is one of your New Testament privileges. If it causes your weak brother to sin, cut it off before him.

You may wonder, then, why Jesus was offending so many. The answer is simple. Jesus offended some people as a result of obeying the Father and serving others. His offense did not come by demanding His own rights.

> Our liberty has been given
> to us for serving and
> laying down our lives.

The Pharisees were offended when He healed on the Sabbath. His disciples were offended by the truth His Father had Him preach. Mary and Martha were offended when He delayed His return to heal Lazarus. But you will not find Jesus offending others by serving Himself.

Paul in his letter to the Corinthians gave this warning:

> But beware lest somehow this liberty of yours become a stumbling block to those who are weak.
>
> —1 CORINTHIANS 8:9

Our liberty has been given to us for serving and laying down our lives. We are to build and not to destroy. Nor was this liberty given for us to heap things on ourselves. Because we have used it in this manner, many today are offended by the lifestyles of Christians. Remember the warning given to us in 1 Corinthians 8:9: "But beware lest somehow this liberty of yours become a stumbling block to those who are weak." Don't allow your liberty to ensnare another—set them free instead.

Adapted from *The Bait of Satan,* 117–125.

Conclusion

The apostle Paul, in writing to the Romans, summed up the heart of God in the matter: "Therefore let us pursue the things which make for peace and the things by which one may edify another" (Rom. 14:19).

Accept His challenge to live as a servant of all.

We should make it our aim not to cause another to stumble because of our personal liberty. What we do may even be permissible according to the Scriptures. But ask yourself: Does it seek the edification of another or myself?

> All things are lawful for me, but not all things are helpful; all things are lawful for me, but not all things edify. Let no one seek

his own, but each one the other's well-being... Therefore, whether you eat or drink, or whatever you do, do all to the glory of God. Give no offense...just as I also please all men in all things, *not seeking my own profit,* but the profit of many, that they may be saved.

—1 CORINTHIANS 10:23–24, 31–33,
EMPHASIS ADDED

I encourage you to allow the Holy Spirit to funnel every area of your life through this Scripture passage. Allow Him to show you any hidden motives or agendas that are for your profit and not for the profit of others. No matter what area of life you might embrace, accept His challenge to live as a servant of all.

Use your liberty in Christ to set others free, not to assert your own rights. That was one of the guidelines of the ministry of Paul, who wrote, "We give no offense in anything, that our ministry may not be blamed" (2 Cor. 6:3).

Adapted from *The Bait of Satan,* 125–126.

Notes

Chapter 2
Lessons From an Unforgiving Servant

1. Margin note, New King James Version (Nashville, TN: Thomas Nelson, 1988).
2. Logos Bible Study Software, version 1.6 (Oak Harbor, WA: Logos Research Systems, Inc., 1993).

Chapter 3
The Trap of Revenge

1. Francis Frangipane, *Three Battlegrounds* (Cedar Rapids, IA: Advancing Church Publications, 1989), 50.

Chapter 4
Seeking Reconciliation

1. W. E. Vine, Merrill Unger and William White, Jr., *An Expository Dictionary of Biblical Words* (Nashville, TN: Thomas Nelson, 1984), s.v. "raca."
2. Ibid.

If you are enjoying the Inner Strength Series by
John Bevere, here are some other titles from
Charisma House that we think will minister to you…

Breaking Intimidation
**Break free from the fear
of man**
John Bevere
ISBN: 0-88419-387-X
Retail Price: $13.99

The Bait of Satan
**Don't let resentment
cripple you**
John Bevere
ISBN: 0-88419-374-8
Price: $13.99

Thus Saith the Lord?
**How prophetic excesses
have hurt the church**
John Bevere
ISBN: 0-88419-575-9
Retail Price: $12.99

The Devil's Door
**Recognize the trap of
rebellion**
John Bevere
ISBN: 0-88419-442-6
Price: $12.99

Pathway to His Presence
**A 40-day devotional
leading into His presence**
John and Lisa Bevere
ISBN: 0-88419-654-2
Price: $16.99

The Fear of the Lord
**Gain a holy fear and awe
of God**
John Bevere
ISBN: 0-88419-486-8
Price: $12.99

Charisma®
HOUSE
Books about Spirit-Led Living

To pick up a copy of any of these titles, con-
tact your local Christian bookstore or order
online at www.charismawarehouse.com.